i never wanted to write a breakup poem

Demetra Nyx

Also by Demetra Nyx:

how to live when the world is dying

Published by Avena Press
Copyright © 2020 Demetra Nyx
All rights reserved.
ISBN: 978-1-7348088-0-3

for my little girl

Introduction

This book will lead you through a breakup that should have been devastating but wasn't, a rapid love affair turned into deep commitment, and a move to a new country. Mostly, though, it is the story of healing my inner critic.

I believe that relationships are some of our biggest catalysts for growth. Relationships show us our wounding, our past patterning. We can continue these patterns in relationship — and we can also heal them in relationship.

We develop pieces of our emotional body through experiences we've had throughout our lives. Often, these pieces cause us to look for qualities in a partner that feel familiar. Usually, these qualities are familiar because they play out the wounding we experienced in our family systems.

Almost every part of this book was written while it was occurring. The dates are almost exact; off sometimes by a week or so, to provide for an easier flow of reading.

Dear Venus,

I want better sex. I want abundance and money that pours into my life. I want so much love and romance and beauty in my life. I want a successful business. I want to be the most enchanting and magnetic person ever. I only want these things if they are in my highest good.

Thank you.

- offering to Venus, early 2019

Liquefy

May

I only avoid writing
When I am avoiding writing about something.

I have all these poems about leaving, and none of them
are helping me with this

My heart is shearing in two and spilling all its fibers
down the river
Pollution, running into the ocean
I never wanted to write a breakup poem

I never wanted to write a breakup poem
Because I thought they were childish
Too cliché, too common
… Basic

I do not know why I need to reach for the sky
Why I cannot be content with enough, why enough is
never enough for me
Sometimes I feel like the only thing guiding me is my
soul
And it feels impossible to not listen to it
This undercurrent of truth
Sometimes I hate my intuition

I play You Don't Get Me High Anymore
on repeat

He says
That's funny

it's funny because our relationship is disintegrating

I brush it off and don't say
anything

He said today that he still felt like things were "off,"
and I said that of course they felt like they were off,
because nothing has changed. He also said he feels like
he doesn't even know how to be intimate toward me
anymore, and now he's not even sure when that started.

I feel like he is not able to understand what I mean
about seeing me more deeply, because he has not gone
there himself. He doesn't really want to go there
himself. And then of course I feel like I'm asking for
too much - and it just goes in circles. I feel like he loves
me so much and I love him so much and it feels like
that isn't enough for me, even though it's enough for
him.

I feel like I am having to watch it all slowly fall apart,
and instead of running away from it I'm having to sit
with it, and it feels terrifying and awful and like the
worst thing in the entire world.

I feel like a horrible person. I feel like this is the third time in a row I've decided someone is not good enough for me anymore. I feel like I would rather be hurt myself than have to hurt someone else. I feel like nobody probably exists who is a combination of all the things that I want.

I feel awful that he doesn't know how to be toward me. I feel like there are not words in the English language to express all of my emotions. It feels like if all the trees in an entire forest collapsed all at once on top of each other and then burnt up.

I do not feel like being alone, I don't feel like living alone and having to do everything by myself. I want to have someone there to wake up next to and fall asleep beside. And at the same time, I wonder if I do actually thrive alone. I'm too independent. I hate when I feel like anybody is restricting me in any way at all.

I feel like there is an invisible thread that guides me through my life, and I do not always get a say in what happens next. Because it feels like sometimes my heart feels so happy in a place or with a person and this thread is all of a sudden like nope sorry actually this is done now and this is the next right step even though it doesn't always make sense to me. And I hate that I always will choose that over my heart.

And also it feels like I must.

I am here and I am listening and I am staying in it, and I also feel like it all hurts so much and it is so unbelievably sad.

I feel afraid that he will come home and not want to work on it anymore, and I feel afraid that he will come home and he will

I also sometimes feel like I am continually chasing something that doesn't really exist, or isn't really worth it. It sometimes feels like what is the point of growth and why can't I be happy just living a more simple life and what if I finally get to a point where I realize actually it wasn't worth it at all and I regret something like not staying with a person who loved me so much. And why do I always have to chase something that feels bigger than myself.

My body already knows. I am already starting the grieving process internally, and I'm not sure if I will stop it. I have been blaming my body for a lot of my resistance to opening up to him sexually lately, and actually it seems like is not my fault after all. It seems the disconnect I have been feeling even within myself is that my body knows something is off.

I feel like if I got really quiet and asked my body is it going to work the answer would be no. And yet I feel this responsibility and desire to give it a chance, to not run away immediately, to stay in it and feel it and notice if he makes a change.

I feel so many opposing things all at one time. When we were talking tonight I felt like I loved him and really wanted to try. Now that we have decided to try, I feel bored. I do want to try to get coaching together but I think I want her to tell us that it won't work. I feel afraid of losing him in my life. I feel like it is the necessary next step.

I feel like who am I to dictate what is the necessary next step

All I seem to do is cry. I cried all day yesterday. All last night. The first thing I did when I woke up was cry. He told me to try to stop focusing on it so much because if all I do is dwell on it while we are trying to work on it that will make it harder. But I just feel like I am grieving.

I feel the same. Caught between the desire for him to work through it all and have it magically be better, and the desire to be with someone who's already in control of their life. I feel terrible for not being more patient with the person that I love. I feel awful. And I still keep having thoughts like… I wonder how I would decorate the apartment if he were not here. And then I see him looking cuddly and I just want to hug and forget about it all.

And also, I don't even know what enough of a reason even is to stay with somebody. I told him last night that being in love is not a good enough reason to stay together and he was surprised. He wanted to know, what would a good reason be? And I don't know the answer to that question but I feel like it is not love. Because I know I love him so much my heart could explode but I also know that I felt that way with my last relationship too. And I think I love people easily.

He told me he realizes he has been taking me for granted today. I can't even tell you how many times I have told him that my main love language is words of affirmation and he has told me that I shouldn't have to have that need. I feel like it is too late for him to decide now that he should have been nicer to me

I don't know if I will ever reread these in the future because they hurt so much to write and probably will hurt to read especially if we break up but I also feel like there is a part of me that is really happy I'm writing this all down so that I can look back at this in such detail later on

June

1

At dusk the flowers smell sweeter
Like goodbye kisses
Or like lollipops

I can wear gray on gray on gray
in LA, and
No one even notices

I leave Venus offerings and they stay there for days
It occurs to me Venus might not like molding tea and
wilting flowers
But I'm into it

She's fucking up my business

I wish I had written more about the decision to end
things with you, but see, it wasn't
Hard.

I mean, I spent days
Waiting for you to go to work
So I could
Scream
Sob
Feel less bad about not pulling myself out of bed

And I wrote things like:

who am I to dictate what is the necessary next step

In my own life

and I thought maybe we could
Work On It
maybe we'd get counseling
maybe we'd get a puppy

But then my pussy thought about being single in LA,
and at least she was rebellious

Because if I didn't have those parts of me
Those I deserve better parts
Those what about the hot, successful men out there
parts
Those I feel bored parts

Then maybe I would have stayed.

But I do
And I didn't

Everybody thinks the secret is this special moment of clarity, of one hundred percent certainty. So they wait for it, and it

never

comes

9

I have been approving of the parts of me that want to write heart-felt missives while starving, because I am spilling over with emotion the way flowers spill onto the sidewalks. Approving of bursting into tears in the middle of the highway because I suddenly remembered a moment from my relationship that was so perfect and beautiful, and I will never have that exact moment again.

Approving of the way I sometimes get so caught up in my own creativity that I cannot break to eat or drink or sleep. Approving not wanting to go to the gym while I go anyway.

Approving of the way that sadness makes me want to immediately board the next plane to any destination I don't know, so that I can feel myself lost in another country where I cannot speak the language and feel the sensation of that very aware moment that happens in the middle of commotion when you realize, I have locked myself out of the house and the locksmith closes in ten minutes and my phone is dying and what will I do if it does, and it brings this form of presence so exquisite that whatever happens seems worth it, to be able to feel this alive in this moment. *I don't know what I'll do then, world,* I think, causing this moment of surrender to nature and other people, which is the deepest form of passion in itself, isn't it, that willingness to surrender.

The choice is anxiety or surrender in those moments and I always choose surrender. The moment when it's like sometimes I think I'm so sovereign but in reality everything is dependent and if you make one little mistake out of your sweet bubble it becomes devastatingly obvious.

Here come the swarms of emotion. Here come the moments that make you feel you are swirling around a whirlpool spiral, coming back to the same things again and again, just different this time. Here come the moments that feel like life is so heart-achingly beautiful that your body longs to be filled with it.

It's like the way you must listen to breathwork music at the gym just to feel the strangeness, like the way chalk mixes with long nails, the way you must long for the grossness of the streets but cry when it all gets to be too much, this not having a forever home or a place to belong and feeling like you will never remove your inner luxury girl, no, not today. You will need this always and you will think this makes you weak, to have to break to go back to big beds with soft sheets and fresh berries and coffee and life. One extreme is no good without the other.

I think of all the hours I spent watching tv shows that I did not want to watch, I did not want to ever waste my time doing. A pattern in all of my relationships, I hear triple voices whisper *why do you only want to watch documentaries*. But I wanted to lie with you and that seemed to be the only way worth doing so that didn't have to lead to sex, anyway.

Not that you ever said that, but I felt it, because how do we get rid of a lifetime of conditioning that quickly? We don't without help, really.

I look at the muscles on my back and their soft ripples are soothing to me always. I think somehow they make me feel cloaked, safe. They stay there even when I am not committed to anything. Even when I have not been to the gym in weeks, there wave the ripples around my shoulder blades.

I think of how my lips are a cross between my mother's and my father's, how I got his coloring except when her olive shades come through and everybody says how did you get so golden brown? And I say I am Greek, you know, even with my blonde hair. I say, you know, northern Greeks had blonde hair and blue eyes, even though I don't know if this is true because it's only been told to me but I want it to be true, because that is the only part of my heritage to which I feel connected.

I think that my biggest pride in my life is that I can sit with my belly bloated and dirty wispy hair and scarred skin and random nipple hairs and say I love you so much, my body and myself, I approve of all of you and nobody else has to approve because I do, and I have arrived now and I am here to stay, I am what you were always looking for and now I am here. I will not leave you.

Approving of the awkward face I make in selfies and approving of the expression I make in dance classes when I do not know the moves, a cross between delight and embarrassment. Approving of all the photos I take of myself after crying, a way to save that moment in time to remember, I can feel hurt this much.

I remember my grandfather's death. I remember sitting in the waiting room while they cut open his chest and tried to open up arteries he hadn't wanted open, but that my mother and uncle insisted he did, because when you have a heart attack at 86 this surgery makes it so that you can live ten more years, and we want ten more years with you. I remember sitting in the room and knowing without wanting to know. So much so that when they said he made it through surgery my body felt surprised - this is not right, she said. But I did not hear, because I said to my subconscious *sometimes you are wrong, it seems.*

And the next day I went to the hospital so he would not be alone and the man who was always so happy to see me, always ruffled my hair and said *you're ok, kid,* that man did not even smile at me. He just held his stupid bright red heart pillow that they give you and he coughed awful sounds and I tried not to think of my brother in the ICU with all the beeping monitors and I said *this is not the same* in my head like a mantra, *this is not the same.*

And my body felt uneasy, and I said no, body, see? He made it through. He is fine.

And then a day later I was flying through the dark roads to the hospital, having left the class I was supposed to teach before it started, because my mother called me desperate, wailing I don't know what happened I don't know if you should come. But I knew, and I went, and he was dead.

And the doctor told the waiting room and everybody was silent but me and so I said, can we see him? Because everyone else seemed mad at the doctor and no one else was speaking. And the doctor said yes, and I went with my mother and I stood there with her while she sobbed "Daddy, daddy" and I said he is dead, that is not him anymore.

He does not exist anymore.

I think about the way that life makes it so that your very sick grandparent survives to make everybody miserable but your healthy-seeming one dies suddenly, and first. I think of how my mother had to lose her son, her husband, and then her father. And how her father was the only parent who really loved her.

Today I saw you, and your beard was long and you said
you were moving to Portland and I felt proud of you

You looked sad. You looked like Portland.

And I felt sad I put that sadness there

I will miss those moments most, unshowered and glasses, early mornings, coffee. I remember how we laid on the salt in the dark, but you were too concerned with taking photos to pay attention to me. All I wanted to do was lie there and talk, looking at the moon and the stars and waiting for the sun to come up, but you did not want to do that.

"This is boring," you would say, about talking.

Talking is not boring to me. All I ever wanted was to hear all of your stories and have you truly hear mine, but you did not know how to share because you did not know what yours were.

I know what mine are. I know every story, every song, every smell that has shaped my life. They are made up of emotion, colors of emotion that I pull out from the air and try on like dresses as they surround me.

I remember every moment in my life through the songs I play on repeat. "We already heard this," you would say as I played a new one, not wanting to learn its significance.

You made me shut off the song that has bonded me to my siblings for forever, because you found it annoying.

One time a boy I had just started seeing asked me to play him some of my favorite music and I thought it was such a beautiful question, though I doubt he realized what it meant to me. He listened so thoughtfully and then he said, "It makes sense to me that you like this," and I felt like that was the best response ever because I didn't really want to know if he liked it, I wanted to know that he understood me through it. That the ribbons of the music tie up my body and pull it around, like puppet strings.

I don't think it would have worked out with him, not really. But I stopped seeing him because I realized I was in love with you.

I think we were too close to not try dating. I remember thinking that we had become so intimate that it would feel dishonest to date another person seriously, while still confiding everything in you.

I used to tell you it felt like you were always reaching over to turn my volume down. *Everything you are, but less,* is what I heard. You said, *you are not too much* and *I feel tired of your dramatic episodes* all in the same breath.

And I was so used to it that I did not notice. It felt familiar, the way relationships do. It felt like I was little and hearing my mother saying you are too messy, my father saying you are too loud, my teachers saying you talk too much. My sister saying, you are annoying. Girls saying, you are intimidating, boys saying you show off too much, you are a slut.

My brother did not act like I was too much. But then my brother was gone

I have been feeling all these words floating in the air around me lately. *Messy. Dramatic. Sensitive. Emotional. Loud. Annoying. Slut. Show-off. Intimidating. Bitch. Talkative.*

They are floating because I haven't decided if I want them yet. All these words, meaning too much of one thing. Not enough of another.

I think I created my feelings of not-enough-ness to mask the wounds of my "too much."

I think my body woke up and I think I knew it in France, where we hit week three of the most miserable stay in Normandy with a misogynistic man and cold rain and my body had hit its maximum tolerance of staying in a situation that was voluntary but you said stick it out, three more weeks, because you were scared. My body was not scared because I trust the world to hold me. I wanted to leave then, but you did not, and I knew then that we were not the same because you tolerate dissatisfaction and *good enough.*

That's life, you say. *Welcome to life.*

And I agreed to stay but my body did not want it so much that the next day the man was so terrible that even you agreed we had to go. You know I created that, right? That my body wanted out and my mind said stay and so the energy around me shifted so strongly that I got what I wanted, without having to make it happen.

Thanks, Jupiter, I whispered as we pulled out of the driveway.

I never want to go back to Normandy.

This is how it happens: I think of a sweet memory and then I remember all the other most irritating ones that I did not allow myself to feel in the moment.

I suppose that is what is like, to slowly let your body fall out of love

Here is the chair that you yelled at me for breaking. It snapped and I said this chair should have been made more strongly and you said, exasperated, why can't you just sit on chairs like a normal person.

I remember when I threw a rock over the cliff and you lectured me like a child, and I stormed down the mountain. I got there first and the ravens sat around me and I said to you *you are not my parent* while they listened.

Here are the nightstands you said you would paint but didn't. Here are the smoke alarms you removed and didn't put back. I saw you took the vodka but not the endless cans of beer, that neither of us drank. I put them in a bag for you. I do not want them

Here is the bedspread that you said had to be blue, even though blue is not pretty enough for my bed. Here is the closet wall you said I could paint but only in the worst combination of colors.

Here is the bookshelf, where finally I will be able to fit my stacks of books

You said you would not help me move the couch. The couch I did not want, because who buys a couch that is denim and not tall enough to sink into at all. There is no purpose in that kind of couch.

I did not need you to help me move the couch. I moved it by myself, and I threw it down the steps and I rolled it down the street, end over end, in my big t shirt and glasses and my hair a mess. You would have laughed to witness it in any other circumstance and I felt sad because that's what you loved about me. But I also felt powerful, because that quality is mine and you do not own it, and you might love it but I love it about myself more

Today it was sunny in LA, and I watched the sky from bed as I gave myself an orgasm and thought about the vibrators I would replace you with

Here is the tree. The tree we bought together and you let me name, since it told it to me. I remember how the tree was very healthy and then suddenly started dying about a month ago. I remember how you said it was because the sun had changed in the sky, but I knew that it was dying because our relationship was dying. And maybe that was its plan with the sun all along

Here is the cast iron pan. I am going to put it away when you leave and never take it out again. I hate cleaning it and you never seasoned it properly. I am going to buy myself a non-stick pan and I will clean it quickly and gently and I will not think of you.

I bought a velvet couch and a pink and purple rug and fake flowers and a gold and marble coffee table and a white bedspread and all the pretty things you said we could not have

Tonight it is the full moon. The moon is in Sagittarius, the same place as my sun. The moon is saying goodbye to you and to all the things that no longer fit me as she begins to wane

You said I should stop singing because I was bad at it
But I did not sing because I thought I was good
I sang because it brought me joy

I do not know how to bring you into my world
Where holding a tomato is like holding a newborn child
Where herbs have feelings
Where the wind and the songs slither through my body
Where the branches wrap their arms around mine

Where everything is so interwoven that it feels
impossible, but also like
of course

He saw my pain and named it true
Saw my extremes and named them gifts

There are boxes and tea kettles and dishes half full of
food
Papers and speakers and foam and sheets
Clothes half dirty and half clean
All in the same pile
Around me

And they do not feel stressful
Because alone, everything happens in perfect time
And the apartment will be cleaned when it is time
And the closet will be organized when it is time
And the food will be cooked when it is time

And I will sit for hours, dried blood on my thighs
Feeling the music fill my body

The breeze comes in to say hello
And it says
You are the flowers spilling onto the sidewalks
You are the superbloom
You are the spicy food you like so much
You are the sunset in a storm

You were never wrong

I feel like I entered another layer of life, like I woke up from a dream. A dream where he was in it and now he is not. The same landscape, just all different.

The fan is spinning around and around and I feel the heaviness in my eyes and it feels like every sensation in my body is so alive.
It happens at this time of night

How can air on my skin, the smell of my underarms, elicit the most pleasurable moans?

Everything is so quiet. The clothes are laughing

I am almost afraid of it. But not really. It feels like I have just stepped out of static.

It feels like, do I make the food or clean the apartment or just lie here, wondering, bleeding

I have begun to sit for hours just existing
I have begun to notice the synchronicities
I think the universe laughs every time it sees my reaction to quadruple digit numbers. *Again?* I never believed in angel numbers. Angels - I rolled my eyes. *Really, again??* I look up and around me as if someone is watching

All of it is watching

There is a song, a Talking Heads song called "And She Was." It was one of my absolute favorite songs when I was little. I felt like the girl in the song (this is a theme for me - I have two songs like this).

I never knew what it meant - I don't tend to listen to lyrics of songs. Just their textures

A few years ago I tried to look it up and could not find an explanation. A couple days ago I googled it and it said:

"Drummer Chris Frantz said of the song, "It's a story about a woman who has the power to levitate above the ground and to check out all her neighbors from a kind of bird's eye view. And the guy who's writing the song is in love with her and he kinda wishes she would just be more normal and, like, come on back down to the ground [Laughs], but she doesn't. She goes floating over the backyard and past the buildings and the schools and stuff and is absolutely superior to him in every way.""

And I thought about how sometimes every moment in time clicks at once

There is a massive tree outside my window and I feel
like it has been watching me always

I say, did you know the whole time?

It says *I just exist, like you are just existing*

I don't want anything you don't want to give me,
universe. But can you give me everything

I wonder about the bleeding, and if it is less painful
because my uterus is breathing a sigh of relief.
Endometriosis is a lack of boundaries, and my
boundaries are stellar, lately

I am writing every day because of you
I am giggling, because of you

I have to edit my writing because of boundaries

The tree says even it has a boundary

July

1

Skype

Took the sheets you slept on
Consecrated them anew
They are infused with my energy, now
And mine alone

He stared at me, powerfully, and I felt him see my soul
My body electrified
Pulsing between my legs, spreading up my back
"Push your hair back," he ordered.
I felt underwater
He told me to touch my own thigh, to say his name, to
moan
He told me to look him directly in the eyes and
penetrate myself
I felt a tsunami in my body

A claw unfurling
Crystals dissolving
The northern lights
My body

"10," he said.
"9"
"Good girl"

All the way to 1, and my body came on command
Rather she
Decided to become the galaxy itself

The ravens sang

My feet and hand fell asleep, my back ached, and it was
hard to notice
Because the water was crashing through
My body, like Andromeda
I gasped

"Tell me you feel safe with me," he said.

I do

3

My body is like spinning cotton candy

Sweetness growing and expanding

I feel like you see straight into my pussy.
Through the screen, no less

There is a wire through the center of my being
I've never felt it before.
It snaps into place from your gaze, my limbs feel the
aftershocks

You are the way the trees look in the morning light

You are a child's excitement on Christmas morning

You are like watching a lion eat an antelope

The silence is on fire

You look at me and my legs open, automatically
I pretend it isn't happening

And yet, I send you my orgasm every time I touch
myself

4

You would think
That if something were to Liquefy
It would need to stabilize and rebuild before it shifted.

But I didn't

I melted myself down
To all the essential pieces
The highest risk, and yet
The most true
I leapt, from that state
Spilled over
Turned into a waterfall
A work of art
An entire ecosystem
Created
By me

Leaping

I noticed today I've stopped using all the words he used
to describe me

Dramatic, extremes

Inconsistent
What was the other one? ——right, emotional

Rewriting the story of my own qualities

Not dramatic, just poetic
Not extremes, just depth
Not inconsistency, just femininity
Not emotional, just able to feel

I am bitter, a little

Tomorrow I am going to get on a plane to meet a man
I might already love

My skin is breaking out and
I feel the kind of no-filter tiredness
that happens right before my period starts

He says he wants to see all of it

I am sitting in a salon, they are cutting dead skin off my
feet and I am feeling like who has a free and wild
enough life that they can book a two-days-away
one-way
plane ticket solely based off of what their body is
feeling

Me

Who falls in love with someone they have not met a
month after a cataclysmic breakup
Who they have had an orgasm with and confessed their
deepest fears to

Me

Feeling like life might not be real, anyway
And if it's not real then money is not a factor
And time is not a factor
And moving schedules is not a factor
And possibilities are not a factor

Because the air is fluid
And it is saying this is what must happen next

It feels like the only thing that has ever mattered

Isn't it always worth it, just to know

15

I'm the shape shifter
That's what you are, too
Genie in a bottle

Taking on a multitude of forms, some
contradicting, all within one being

It's my favorite thing about myself
It's my favorite thing about you

There are 8 divergent pathways and we've
gone down each one

I hit play on babe I'm gonna leave you
Like an apology

The orchestra is playing
Tires hitting runway

Zeppelin, Mozart, fucking
crescendos in my ears

Seeing you for the first time was not magic, it was
strange
Like the winds were changing colors
Like puzzle pieces of time had collided
and needed a moment to recalibrate
The plates of the earth were shifting

You were the same, and different
than I imagined
Or maybe it was that all my fears got called up to the
surface
and I knew you could read them on my face, so I had
to name them.

Insecurity, one
Do I like you, another
You will see right through me, a third
I can't hide from you like I can hide from others

You were calm. And my body settled

Your tears are like springtime
the way they impact my body

Your orgasm, snapping jaws
Or a black hole

I've never seen someone more mesmerizing.

Your eyes hold my greatest potential
Like running river water
Like truth or dare

Your body turns mine to putty
I am perfume around you

I want all of your childhood memories
I want all of your stories in my body

You dance and the sky smiles

Here I am

in love with you

Sometimes it feels like I could vibrate right out of my
body
Like the boundaries of my skin are not that clear
Like my energy is liquid
Like if I just closed my eyes I could merge with
everything at once

Sometimes it feels like I am pink puffs of smoke in the
sky
I am every crow in every tree
Sometimes I see myself dancing
Even when my body is still
Sometimes my body is the person across the street
And the bike they are riding on
And the street getting touched by the bike

Sometimes all matter is music in solid form
Sometimes even triggers feel erotic

Everything is alive because it is dying

All of these moments. I want to lick them like the last drop of soup from a bowl. I want to be so immersed in every second. Like I am a fireplace. My body is made up of gratitude.

You, like cherries.

You, making me breakfast in your underwear.

You, with your deep sounds. Laughing at your own jokes.

I feel dropped into love with you. It is as if somebody pushed me underwater and I turned into a mermaid. It is like life wanted me to have a physical sense of what home feels like and it presented me with you.

I trust all of your decisions. I want to hand you the keys to all the decision-making. I want to add flavor and that's all. I want to write and dance and laugh and fill up the honeypot that you have shaped so carefully.

My pussy drips for you. I have never felt such grounded sexual desire.

I am in surrender to you but mostly to all of life right now, it seems. Following pleasure moment to moment. Following my desire. Life says, move countries, sell all your things, move in with someone you've just met and these things don't sound illogical to me because I have never felt so home.

I want everything with you. Mostly I want all of the mundane moments. I want to hear you draw out an unfunny joke forever. I want to watch you dance to yourself. I want to watch your face as a new thought enters your mind. I want to watch your eyes darken when you're thinking sexual thoughts. I want to spill things all over the floor and have you not react, just laugh at me. I want to feel you drink me in, be nourished by me.

I want to lie naked in bed with you. I want to be drowning in your smells, in the cologne you put on your tummy because of how tall you are. I want to put my mouth on your cock, all the time, not even in a sexual way but just because I love it and want it there. I want to feel you get hard just from me telling the truth.

It sounds like he didn't like cuddling, you say

No, he liked cuddling. He would just get... bored. And he didn't really want to touch unless it led to sex.

So it sounds like he didn't like cuddling.

We cuddled.. I think. Did we?

I guess he didn't like cuddling.

I think of all the times I did not like cuddling and all of the men who did not touch me like you.

When it was taking me a long time to orgasm I felt the remnants of others not caring, and him demanding, "what do you *need*," as if something was wrong because it was taking so long, today. And I would not be able to describe with my language. Because sometimes my energy just does what it does.

I said to you, I feel like I am taking too long, and you so gently laughed with such love and you said *no one is timing you. I get so much pleasure from your pleasure. This feeds me, just watching you.*

And I tried to soak that in.

I felt the patience in your body and when I finally came your hands stayed there afterwards, caressing my hip bones, stroking my thighs, gently over my pussy again, just like you loved to feel my body. Just like you loved me, and were infusing me with love. And then I cried, because I had never been touched like that before. I would have said some of my partners were patient but they were not patient in this way, in a way where they get pleasure from my pleasure, in a way where my body is fascinating. I always wanted someone to look at me that way.

I thought I was demanding too much

Tell me about life, about the ways our paths have somehow intertwined and we are moving along as one

These contented sighs, they feel like nectar to my body. Like valium, or what I imagine valium would feel like. A sinking into my own body. Your arm goes up and mine does too. You take a deep breath and I feel my body following before I even know it. You say the thought I was just thinking. I don't even point it out because it feels so constant.

Like the angel numbers. Like the synchronicities too weird to be coincidences. Like the way everything is bursting glitter in the air.

Your big hands on my thigh. You laugh like a little boy in one moment, and then you say "In my room" as a direct order and my energy drops immediately. You tell me what I like and what to do and my body submits to you. So willingly. It feels so natural.

It feels like, here is life. And I hear the sounds of traffic and feel my body on your carpet and my eyes want to shut from the sleepiness of constant 2 am nights and so many tears and still. Still. I feel exquisitely present to all of it.

I want to hear all of the moments you've felt uncertain, insecure. I want to watch you tell them to me with a hesitancy in your eyes. It feels like you are asking in those moments, *do you still love me like this* - and like my body floods with the purest adoration for you.

Of course I do.

I don't know what to do with a love like this, where we are so integrated you are not triggering the wounding I am used to. Instead you are uncovering the depths of my wounds around my father, around men. It feels like I am scraping out the insides of my body and like my body is saying, yes, what else is not light.

25

I started crying and the sky started pouring in the
darkness

I opened up my entire heart. I said, these are all the
ways you trigger me.

I said, these are all the ways men have hurt me, have
disappointed me. These are the ways I haven't fully let
people in, ever.

These are the secrets I haven't told anyone.

These are all the reasons I am terrified of being loved
by you. These are the reasons parts of me want to push
you away.

As I closed my eyes and sobbed the hardest, lightning
flashed and it rained harder.

You said, it never rains like this in Vancouver

My tears hit my hair and my bare breasts and I felt like
I was the entire earth, crying

You held my eyes and said, these parts of you do not
scare me. I love you more, now. Thank you for sharing
your truth.

Thank you for sharing your truth

You said, loving you is not work for me.

I wiped my tears and the rain slowed. The glow from the salt lamps filled the room. And we lay on our bellies, staring at the rain through the window

26

The first time you entered me, my womb was my body
and it was like I disappeared into space
It felt like my body was a portal
It wasn't desire
It was a need to be filled.
It felt like that was the only next thing that mattered.
That my body wanted your body in me
It felt like it had nothing to do with me or you, really
Just an energetic necessity

If we were made up only of colors, and the colors were
all waving together
and then blue and red mixed long enough that they had
to make purple
That was what it felt like

And you asked your body, and your body felt ready
And as I felt you in me
I cried

What other response is there

I am on my knees to life

August

4

You said you trusted me to write about whatever you brought to me. And yet here you are, with this bullshit.

I demand higher for you than this.
I demand more for you than this.

There is a man lying here who has been burning in the sunshine, passed out by the ocean.
Now he is playing the ukulele

I want everything with you. I have never felt so in flow with life. It feels like we have infinite work to do together, and the time to start is now.

My friend said life is precious. You know?

You told me to trust my body so fully, but you are not trusting your body.

Maybe I know because I asked for this. I said Venus, please give me everything that is in both of our highest goods, and she delivered. And you are saying, wait, actually, maybe I would like to control it.

You don't get to control life. That's not how she works.

The tide is coming closer to my feet because it wants to touch me

I am hungry but I don't want to eat because look at this, right in front of me. The seaweed matted to the rocky sand. The ocean having an orgasm. The branches reaching for the water. The sun being a spotlight on the water.

Me in my long skirt, braless, staring at the ocean

If you say no to this, I will know you are not in alignment with life and I will take these gifts and I will not want to be with you anyway, because how could I be with someone who did not trust life.

The mountains are tolerating the city

What are you telling your friends? Have you not told them how you sob to me at night? Have you not told them how we have spoken our fears out loud? Have you not explained the healing?

My friends all trust me

I felt aggravated when you brought this to me because it was the first time I had seen you not act like you. You are getting caught in a story. You are acting all suspicious.

I am not afraid of losing this connection. Because I do not want it if it is not aligned. And it no longer would be if you paused it

I felt like a puppy, licking your face while you were laughing, and then suddenly you screamed no and put me on a leash.

I felt my father, giving me alcohol and then yelling at me when I got in trouble for drinking it

The man with the ukulele has passed out again, with it on his lap.

The reason people say to wait before moving in together is because most people do not spend the first three weeks of dating being together 24/7 and processing their deepest wounding.

I do not feel afraid that there is anything you could realize about me that you did not know.

Do you? Do you have things about you I do not know?

I know your feelings before you say them, so I doubt it

The sky is exploding with fireworks for us and you are saying wait, stop the excitement, the beginning should have been slower. But the show has already started

All of life is ready to celebrate us. What are you doing?

You said you trust me to write about whatever things you bring me. Well here it is, on a page

6

Thank you for your tears

Thank you for your humbleness, for your willingness to
sit in front of me and express your shame
Thank you for knowing your stories
Thank you for knowing how to center yourself and
return back to your body
That ability is earned, I know

Thank you for your ease, for being willing to sit with
my reactions
Thank you for trusting my body
Thank you for trusting your body

When you expose yourself to me
When you are most vulnerable
My body softens

That is what allows me to open

It is like a flower in the sunshine
Gentle, steady
Responsive

I
also
slip into my stories

They are:

I like to feel misunderstood
So special
that I am non-understandable
So complex
I am exhausting to figure out

Too witchy, too much pain, too many layers
to be worthwhile of explaining
it is easier to feel
Queen of drama
than to let you hold me
Understand me
in all of my emotions

I have been wounded by all men forever
I will never heal my body
Eventually you will get sick of me
I ask for too much

sometimes I am so invested in being mean to myself,
that
when you love me through my frustrations and my
tears, it is too much to bear and so I must push you
away and feel resentful
to let you love me I'd have to love myself,
and that would kill the story.

The last time I was on a plane, I was sweating
Full of apprehension, and not knowing
It felt like the air might not hold me and I'd just
dissolve before I arrived

Now I am on a plane and I feel....... fine

My heart broke all of yesterday, I suppose
like I was missing you preemptively
My whole body felt sad
until you entered me this morning
I remembered energy can stay connected

Now that I am on the plane I feel....... fine

Curiously, I feel motivated
happy for the space
Let me sell my life away
I wanna live with you forever

I miss my pink rug, and my couch covered in velvet
I miss LA flowers
I will land and see the palm trees
I will take long baths and blast music in my own
solo
apartment

I wonder if these things will be enough to keep
from missing you

Everything in my apartment must go.

It is not that hard to go through everything after all, I am finding. I am letting go of all the remnants of my old self.

I have decided to have a funeral for myself. All the old photos - me as a baby, me drunk in high school, me dancing on a table and with old boyfriends and in old places.

Burn them all. I'll have my own ritual, and it will be wild.

My body makes no sense to me but I love her anyway. One moment she feels so exhausted that our thoughts come out in jumbles, or we are silent. Then I turn the music on and drink water and she is like right, this is what we were needing all along, and she starts moving like the waves in the ocean.

I want to be in an epic story of letting go. An extravagant fairy tale, where there is an old witch who cackles and a woman with the longest hair and thoughts all made of string. It must be glorious, or nothing.

He said he loves how ravenous I am — for all of life.

I feel that is what I am doing, sometimes. Gulping life down my throat.

I was in an enchanted forest this week where the trees

looked like a Disney set, but they were not a Disney set, they were real. Thousands upon thousands upon thousands of years old, they told me we are all already rich in experience, in knowledge, in what we have seen.

The roots of these trees were so big that they created an interwoven network with one another, sharing intelligence, keeping connected. I imagine them holding hands, twisting, creating an entire underground world of community.

I am drinking chaga and greens because I've only eaten bread products the past 48 hours and that is good for me, right?

I am drinking chaga and greens and washing the dishes and writing two things and dancing and going through my things, all at once.

Tell me about the moon, and the ocean, and tell me how they want me closer to them all the time

My apartment is filled with dead flowers and plants, mostly

What should I do with all my shoes? I feel like all my clothes are moments in my life, and I don't think I want them anymore.

The first time I ever had sex—

—not the time I lost my virginity, since virginity is a made-up thing that does not actually exist, since my

body and my sex and my value are not things I can
lose—

—he called me by my best friend's name and fucked
me with the TV playing in the background.

I am wondering if I can print out the photos of all the
men who have ever been inside me, and burn them out
of my body

Do you know what I think of every time I'm in a movie theater?

Mass shootings

This walk has been without constellations

Flat keys on ice

sometimes I get really quiet and I listen.

My apartment is clean, and it's not mine. My truck, my
baby, my safety net — disappearing. Getting sucked
back into the consumer void.

It meant something to me

it won't to them. my flowers, my paint, my
grandmother's items. nothing will mean things
anymore.

They will mean new things, maybe, but probably not. It
is like the way people stare at nature in parks without
seeing. nobody feels things anymore

I had a funeral for myself and I no longer exist

I want to cover myself in spices and lie in the middle of
the floor.

I am shaving off layers of me
peeled and raw and rare
If the world is a sponge I am afraid of being absorbed

it feels like if I let go of all of these things, there is
nothing to stop me from blending
like my items are rooting me
who are we when we are left with only our bodies

But there is no one to tell me I am being dramatic, so I get
to blast songs and blend
with the breeze from the fan
drinking mushrooms and not eating

interlude

Sweet girl
You might not belong to their eyes
But you belong to the universe

That might not be a consolation
that you are like the sunset over sunset boulevard
you are like the burning amazon

it's like: your body is there, and here are
you

They've lied to you

your dreams aren't gonna come from the certificate
or the pay increase
or the husband and the baby

your dreams are in the hot
container of your womb

in the parts you don't understand
between your thighs

they're in the feeling of the air tickling your skin
of the snotty breakdowns of despair
in the times you yell too loud, with your joy

Your orgasm has the power to break the ceiling
Your expression … water
Your pleasure is the force that moves everything

your discomfort with these parts is what you've been
taught to believe

run your fingers up your thigh and notice
how that feeling is for you

Touch your hair — yours

look at the bumps on your skin and wonder
who benefits from you feeling like that
is
wrong

Sweet girl

You should have learned at ten
the miracle your body had inside

Then it would not have been shut down or hidden
away
you would not have spent hours on the internet,
searching
Your pleasure would not have been
taboo

Your thoughts are creating what's around you

Look

what if: the air was alive

what if everything was more magical and mysterious
than you ever thought possible

It is

It was never really lived in, anyway

There was never a table for the record player
No holes put in walls

No cushions for the chairs, or
jars labeled with types of flour

There were only half-put-together
Things

you
were
never
going
to
stay

In retrospect, this makes sense
You didn't want sex
because he tore you
down

you bought things you didn't like
that
much

But you blamed yourself, 'cause it
was
easier

But sometimes, my love

it is not about
you
And it is more about
what
he
lacks

The altar is torn down, now
The calendar, ripped from the wall

how do you put a life into four boxes?

You'll put things on the sidewalk
with a sign that says "free"
You will heat cold pizza in the oven
You will look around at empty space
it will be swept clean, and there will be no trace of
You

What is home, anyway
if it is not a collection of things in a place

I was sitting on the pavement behind my building,
barefoot next to the dumpster, in a long black dress I
had worn in April at a wedding. I was having a funeral
for myself, I was burning seventy photos of my old life
in a bowl that was spun by a person in Pittsburgh,
Pennsylvania. There were slits up each leg, the dress fell
around my thighs. The flame burst each time I lit a new
image. The air smelled like acid. It was just me, the
photos, the bowl, a candle, a paper scrawled with my
handwriting, and my phone, softly playing songs from
2000. And a man who must have been watching out his
window decided he was entitled to approach the girl
sitting on the ground near the dumpster and he walked
outside with a glass of wine as if she would take an
open drink or any drink or put her mouth on a glass
that came from a strange man who had been watching
her burn photos from his window with no care for
interrupting something

sacred

September

Vancouver, I see blue skies today
but my mood is black
and foul

He is smothering

is it that I cannot accept love
or am I gaslighting myself
blaming me when it's really
him

I lasted 5 days and then I left to find my own place

Everything feels repulsive

It feels like the universe is laughing at me
Haaaaaa
here is what you thought you wanted
don't you want it??

My vulva mug
My altar bowl
My pretty five thousand dollar clothes
that don't fit

Let me surround myself in things and pretend I am
home

The thing is that I trust life so much
that it can feel impossible and I am still like
this is for me

so what am I missing

Business is booming

in theory

Do I want to be rooted, or
do I want to fly to a random island in Colombia

the problem is there is no escaping myself

LA was my favorite but I don't like it anymore
He smiles and my body recoils

Does it not feel perfect because I didn't know how it
could be?
Because I was waiting for it to fail?
or because this is not what I wanted, after all

It feels wrong to leave
I want to cry tears of rivers
tears
of
rivers
To be in an unfamiliar city used to be the best thing

"Do you want my love," he says
and to me it registers as a threat

I don't know
maybe I was doing better before

The universe is laughing
Here is everything you could have ever wanted

is it?

I want him to pull me in and say everything's ok
I want my head on his chest, my cheek to feel the
warmth

Too much fire, it said
I am wondering if I was blind

Here is the sun, Vancouver

I don't feel it

I want to cry but I can't
I want to clean but I want to collapse into bed

Everything feels terrible and scary. I feel like I got here and it is the complete opposite of what I imagined it would be. I feel like what if I don't like him after all. Sometimes I cannot stand his high opinion of himself and the way he treats me like a child and it feels classic, like all the things I thought were cute are now not cute at all. Here we are, in the power struggle, and it feels like everybody else was right.

Why didn't we have a honeymoon phase? Did it not feel like infatuation because that's a good thing, or because we are not that compatible?

I don't want to have this pattern forever, of what - of not being able to find a partner? Is it that I am just going through a breakup, and now I am dating?

I am growing, a lot

I did a great thing by slowing myself down. I am actually freer than ever. I can pack my bags and leave at any time. Nothing has changed. Besides that I no longer own my things and I am running out of money again since I spent it all on clothes, and I am running a blowjob class that is making lots of money but that I have no clue what to talk about because I was supposed to practice on the man I don't want to touch, right now.

I can lead a blowjob class without him, whatever

I literally have no clue what I am doing at all

but I do.

Let me eat the chocolate you bought for me, thank you
Let me message the followers you got me, thank you

It feels like everything is pointless, anyway

I don't want anyone in my space. I don't want anyone
near me. I like my aloneness. I like my Self.

I think I love him

The sun is starting to look more friendly
I think of my hand in his hair
I think of his stories

Feels like I threw up all over the page and felt better
fucking storm, Vancouver

Let me feel the city lights
Let me feel the lightening
Let me feel the blood between my legs

My blood is late, this month

This is what it looks like to adapt

I feel Lifted

little boxes of apartments
little lives on display
a lady in a red dress
a lady in a black shirt
a man on the balcony of his penthouse
a man putting on his jacket

Let me
Buy
More
Things

Let me surround myself in things and pretend I am
home

One song on repeat
Predictable changes

Sometimes it feels like there is a magnet that switches
on and that's when I land back in myself.

It is like, the clouds are moving quickly and that
building looks vacant but it is full of live
ones

My favorite spaces are wide open and empty
fields
The vastness of Death Valley
airplanes in the sky
Fill it by existing

The clouds are low, and I
like it

I will stay here forever, in this place
People watching from my window
A city has never been so perfectly stimulating
gentle pressure

There is an American flag next to a Canadian flag
am I in a new country or the same place
it is jarring

I want to fill up every inch of this apartment
I want to strip in front of the window
walls
I want to play music and listen to the clock tick
I want to feel my hip dig into the mattress

I want your mouth on mine, I want to walk down the
street together, laughing

I want to feel free and here at the same time

It never ceases to amaze me how easy it is to settle in a place. Land somewhere new. Google an apartment. Set up the bowl, the mug, the candles. Feel held, and at home.

But at the end of the day it is just me and you, Earth. So that's how I must settle into a place. Alone

He used to tell me I could not say I love you to him
during sex or immediately afterward. It would ruin the
meaning, or something. So I bit my tongue over and
over and I taught my body this is Wrong, and it only
has meaning sometimes. That somehow the act of sex
is not to be trusted, because it could make you say
things that were true at other times but could not be
also true in this moment, because sex was Bad and was
not about love. or maybe too much love in those
moments would have been too much, and I
acquiesced because this made sense, didn't it things
men say make sense

I did not think I would feel landed in this place.

It seemed like too much at once. Too much stimulation, too much change. All of my things ripped away and gone. No more people holding me to my old life. Friends cut away. My dresses, my couch, my car, everything. Gone.

but actually I feel better. The shock of it all had to dissipate while I understood my new space. While I began to feel the way my body blended with this place, this city, this country. The way I navigate myself, here.

In LA I found myself forced to self-sufficiency. It felt like there were so many things to take care of, I realize now. There were bills. A lease I signed. Car insurance. Everything was effort. The heat was effort. Getting food was effort. The expectation of home was effort.

Even when I left a place, some of my life was elsewhere

Maybe I do not want to own any things.

When I landed here I felt like my system was frozen. Unfamiliar, boxes.

Now there are no boxes. Now I have put myself in a space. I do not own the couch, the pots, the pans. The energy is clean, because they are no one's. It is like a hotel. I can just adapt to them.

It is my favorite thing, to take a temporary space and make it feel like home.

I feel curious about myself, mostly. The way one thing feels true and then the same thing doesn't.

I will never, ever, ever
get tired of looking out this window. There is something that is nourishing to my entire body in a way I never expected, to see calm city lights, big, spacious buildings, aliveness. Everything feels happy in my body.

None of these things, I own. Now all I own is my few bags. My business, online. My flowy pretty dresses. I bought things for the rain and I made the rain fun.

It does not feel stressful, to do laundry or cook or clean in a place I do not own.

Everything feels calm. I did laundry today. I stared out the window all day. I watched how the forecast says rain but it really does not rain all day, in this place. The clouds come in low and they move so quickly, and the light shifts in pretty ways, and sometimes it rains when it's sunny and sometimes it's clear when it's cloudy.

No gym in weeks and I love my body anyway

I do not own a car. Not owning a car had been unthinkable because car meant freedom. But actually, money means freedom, and money means renting a car, or having others drive me around, or paying for transportation.

All of my things are with me in one place and I am not even attached to the place.

My body had been frantic with these feelings. Of not feeling rooted. All last year, for eight years, really, there was constant travel, constant stressing out. When would I find a place where I would stay in one spot and settle. I felt like I had been avoiding connection, by running from things and not staying in a place.

But I think really I had been running from myself.

Moving from place to place, to get distracted and excited by places, to get turned on by the way they made me feel about myself. But not feeling at home in myself. Even in LA, buying things, signing things, to make a relationship feel more like home. And then trying to make a solo apartment feel like home.

How to make things feel like home

I do not think it has ever been that I am afraid of commitment. I don't think I have ever been afraid of that.

I also do not think I was tired of movement, of things that were temporary. Not really.

Both of these things feel the same now, really. The desire for constant change. The desire for constant stability. Both are a way of avoiding feeling completely present and at home and believing in myself.

I think I have been looking for external markers, trying to find certainty, trying to trust the world around me so I did not have to fully trust myself.

Being self-sufficient felt tiresome. It felt masculine, like a schedule, like a lonely thing to master. It even felt lonely in LA.

Now it does not feel like that. It feels like ease. Like I can provide for myself in any changing moment, that circumstances can shift and here I am, still, at home in myself.

Gone is the urge to constantly move around, to go to new places in search of myself. Gone is the urge to run away. Gone, also, is the urge to root down.

It just feels like I don't need anything, actually. Like whatever I have ever needed is just here in my own body. Like I have myself, and I trust my ideas, and I trust the way one idea leads to another to a magical occurrence I could have never predicted. I trust the way my body looks at airbnb listings and does not read details, just feels the truth and says, this one. This one, this one, this one. All choices made easy, if we listen.

Oh, it does not have to feel like a Big Deal. Oh, I am just a woman suddenly free from made-up attachments, who trusts her ability to navigate life with ease.

I like Vancouver. It feels weirdly void of provoking things in me. It feels like the mistiness just holds me.

Every city has an energy, and every place in the world seems to affect the way I feel in myself.

Here I just feel supported

I am not really worth any of this. The attention has been broken, Instagram deleted, and I am forgotten.

It wants to pull me down and I am only half willing.

There are things to *feel*, and even for someone whose career is based on feeling, the idea of feeling is exhausting.

Can we transform connect alchemize

I don't know

I open my lap and the words fall out

When all of life feels tired, that's when I know I have not been true to myself.

I am avoiding Feeling, and that is Important

It's …….. empty

I ask her to be my friend, she doesn't answer and *see she doesn't want to be my friend anyway I should never reach out to people first she was lying about liking me and faking it as always all women do people are so annoying because no one has good boundaries I don't even want to be her friend I should make sure she knows I don't actually like her that much and I don't care that she doesn't want to be my friend because I don't even need friends and don't even really like her anyway*

I feel lonely, and like I should not want to sleep in bed with him every night. I should preserve myself, I think. I should keep my freedom cold in case I need it back, and soon. Anything could go wrong at any time.

Not wanting to sleep alone feels like a warning sign, it means things are dangerous and wrong. CAUTION, it blares red in my head
You are beginning to lose your alone-ness, and it is not SAFE

he could die

I should keep my apartment and not live with him

I feel afraid of stepping into everything fully.

No thank you, to practices. No thank you, to ideas of doing anything that will help.

Let me sit here and watch the clock tick by until it is too late to do anything effective

All I want to do is lock myself up and write poems

Today, I feel like

Today, I feel like feeling sorry for myself

Rooting

October

I've been so good about speaking up for my desires.
Yes, space. Yes, this tea. Yes, dessert.
No, not like that.

So much processing. So much healing.
but we are getting better at it

Let's get plane tickets, so we can have a Pennsylvania
white christmas and we can sit by the fire with my
family

I am in Vancouver. I am with a man I love, and I have
moved countries.

Your soft back like the moon against my fingers
You fill my mouth you fill my e n t r a n c e
My body begs for you
drips for you
You have owl eyes

My body is unraveling, untying knots
You've pulled on the end and
the whole ribbon came undone

My body, unwrapping
My body, a flame

You growl and my body crumbles
becomes dough

Tell me what to do with it

My mind, a fence
topples over

I belong to you, I say

Sir

I feel ancient with you
Like we are in all times at once
Like I have been looking into your eyes like this for
hundreds of thousands of years
Like it is about so much more than us.

Your back an animal
You slip between my legs
then
My tongue on velvet
You love yourself I love you
r body your mind your heart
you down my throat
I will choose not breathing to be filled by you

what do I taste like?

like taking a drink of nature

what do I smell like?

the ocean

why do you like her?

she responds like another mouth. swelling, opening, like a woman

Let's buy plane tickets
Let's go to Paris
Let's have sex for a week in sunny
places
and in rainy ones

Thank you, apartment
feels like you have served your purpose
already

Why do you think some flames dance and some stand
tall?

I can be with your kindness when I
am being kind to myself

16

My heart felt expanded, opening

Will you kiss me? he asked gently

I moved my mouth down between his legs

and I kissed softly, leisurely. And then I sat up.

I ran my hands over his thighs, his belly, his cock. As slowly as I wanted. Noticing the silkiness of his skin, various moles, the shape of his body.

Appreciating. Adoring. Feeling my own pleasure in what I touched.

Minutes passed.

We gazed at each other, in love.

I asked if he wanted me to keep touching him like that, or if he would prefer my mouth.

"I don't think I'll know until you try," he said.

Again, so gently with my mouth. Love flowing from my mouth into his cock.

Everything, so slowly.

I began dripping. I could feel it all over the bed, all over my own legs.

I kept moving love into his body.

Maybe centuries went by, I don't know.

"Can I be inside of you?" he asked

I said of course

As I moved to lay on top of him, tears started running down his cheeks.

"Is this okay?" he asked softly.

The real question - are men allowed to open, too

"Yes," I said. "I am so in love with you

My whole body is begging for you inside of me."

Are you ready?" I asked.

"Yes," he said.

We looked into each other's eyes.

He entered me, and we held still.

My vagina, like my fingertips. Every part feeling energy, the slightest sensation. Like my body electrified. Like someone had hit the key code and a door I didn't know existed suddenly started to open.

My body, expanding inside. My cervix, opening. Like my vagina was widening, lengthening, to depths I didn't even know she had available.

My body, pouring shimmers of love from my chest.

He filled me, and we moved slowly. I felt tears well up in my eyes. I did not force them out. Every part of me felt a complete surrender to our energy.

We followed the energy. It came in waves: gentle, aggression, softness, connection.

And then my body came - so softly, exquisitely, valley orgasms expanding through every part of my body.

Our bodies blending into one another. Endless tingling.

My insides felt open. Everything felt open, like I did not have physical barriers at all. It felt like somebody went into my vagina and gently released her from the cage that had been keeping her small.

I came again, from his mouth. He came from my mouth. His body shaking.

We complimented each other's bodies.

We laid there, in love

I feel like I am getting on an amusement park ride, on a
roller coaster that might take me anywhere, and I don't
know what will happen.
but I'm finally boarding one. This one! I don't care
where it goes, I've never been more certain about
anything in my life.
It sounds fun

Your eyes are the night sky
They are like polished wood in the sunshine

I am resting, resting
We are like unwinding laffy taffy
We are peeling back pieces from bones
We are saying what else haven't we shared, yet
What else is there to know

I have been eating fun dip
Dunking white sugar in blue
it tastes like the boardwalk
It feels nice, doesn't it,
at least for a minute
it tastes like being little

I think about how I did this. How I moved so many
feelings through my body. How I sent out orgasms to
the universe. How I resourced into pleasure. How I
trusted myself, over and over

It feels dangerous to claim that we create anything for
ourselves

We move into an apartment next week that is the most perfect fit we could have found. Everything happening so smoothly, over and over again.

This morning my stomach hurt and he massaged my feet and we found a spot that hurt so badly, and we laughed and said what if this was the stomach reflexology point, lol wouldn't that be funny, and we looked it up and it was

Why is the sun so pretty
My fingerprints match the trees
My vulva matches flowers
My fingers pucker in the water so I can grip fish better, apparently
Sea otters splash in the ocean
The wind blows the chairs across the deck
Why am I so pretty

I have been learning so many lessons about business. Having to fire, having to hire. Discovering how to make lots of money in one day, and then having my social media banned. It feels like life is like, you've learned this, now learn it in a different way. I am open to it

I am not hungry
I am hungry for life, instead
Let me suck the salt out of the air
Let me hear the tear drops

The palm trees don't belong here
The bats swoop
I feel both afraid and happy

You haven't played guitar, yet
You haven't fucked me intensely
Maybe I need to soften

Let me open to you
Let me melt into the couch
Let me become a blanket

November

This is how you Rest, during Winter:

Look at website traffic. Look at followers going up, without effort.

Cry, because years ago your family did not understand why you were so sad, and they still do not

Sleep, a lot. Wonder why you are feeling so heavy, so sad. Get annoyed that resting is a thing that must occur, for anything, at any time, in all of nature.

Roll your eyes at the man being so loving and kind to you, because you are committed to a bad. mood.

How dare he not realize that you are committed to feeling bad today

Coach others. Feel that fill up your heart. Feel how that is something you can be proud of - how you are emotionally capable, now, of taking care of yourself so well that no matter what you are feeling you can pause to hold clear space for someone else

Cook. Cry about how he criticized everything you did, constantly. Cry about how "being easy to make fun of" was so highly valued when you were little. Cry about how you have internalized that as an inner self critic

Notice how spices blend together and what it tastes like when you do not add enough salt

Notice how 8 years of constant adaptation, travel, change .. has not allowed you to fully turn inward

Consider how you cannot turn inward because you have a responsibility to post

More! more! more! Production

Consider how you do not have any responsibility because everything is pointless

and also remember how the world is burning?

Try not to buy things
Roll your eyes at consumerism
Decide to be a minimalist

Spend $10k on various household items
and be nowhere close to done

Set up your Home. Order the most beautiful plates. Three of the eight will not quite match the rest, because it's mercury retrograde and that's how this move is going

Ask the girl who missed her deadline for your money back. Again, in a different way. It's mercury retro for everyone, and those who don't do business well shouldn't be in business

Skim 300 messages a day about the money shame of other women. We are all drowning in shame. Now we are outing shame. She says, shame is adorable

Self pleasure. Squirt onto a blanket. Feel your eyes well up with tears because of how incredible your capacity is for pleasure. Get a burst of energy

Shower for the first time in three days

Dark blue is the worst color for a bedspread. Notice how it seems to follow you everywhere, mocking you - your home cannot be feminine

Agonize over bedspread choices for five hours
Order a plain white bedspread
Order a plain white bedspread and pay extra to ship it to Canada

Wonder about femininity. You are enjoying cooking and cleaning and making the house smell nice. Everyone is laughing at you - you are not a real feminist. You are not like those pathetic women who love baking

So what are you, then??

Read about new training programs. Feel overwhelmed by the thought of integrating anything new.

No more new

Go to therapy. Go to therapy and sit on the couch of a woman with grandmother energy.

She will say, it sounds like your system is all changed out

and now you are finally getting some time to really feel
And rest

She will say, I think it's time you told the story of your
grief. Let's go through it,
piece
by
piece

She will say, I see an unusual strength, here

And you will cry.

Because, you have things coming out soon and the
world only values people being constantly in their
summer

But it seems like winter is finally here and it is not
taking any prisoners, just you

I am in a cocoon. A cocoon of white linens and dark brown wooden tables and his scent and messy hair. A cocoon of too much sleep and not much else getting done. A cocoon of leaves falling, rain spilling, baths being drawn.

The season is fall and I am in winter.
Maybe I am in both, at once, simultaneously, like vines wrapping around a tree.

I laid naked in the forest the other day. Clenched the dirt under my fingertips. Cried into the moss and the soil.

A naked body, trees for miles. Curled up. Leaves in hair.

She looks at me, she says: he never met a lot of your needs, it sounds like.

I don't know if he met a lot of my needs, I say.

What needs does a father meet for you, anyway?

What does a father do?

Sometimes, I have sex with Jordan and I cry and at the end it feels like someone has reached down into the earth and plucked me up and brought me into a room that is white, all white. Where the sound comes in and out, like when someone almost dies in a movie. But it is soothing. There are lots of voices, and they are all faded. I feel his body on mine and I hear all the voices and see a hand passing over my forehead and the voices say you can rest now, it's okay, you're safe here.

And I wonder if this is real, because life up until now has never felt like it could be this good, and like it doesn't feel right for things to be this perfect, and who really gets to have this great of a life, and I wait for what will go wrong next.

I've felt pretty bored. Or still - is there a difference?
I've felt like the online world is going by without me.
I've noticed the colors of the different leaves during
fall. I've noticed how the cold air feels nice on my skin.
I've noticed how I can breathe when it rains and how
easy life is when it's sunny.

I've noticed all the deepest emotions around my family
get pulled up by the root, with dirty, capable hands.

Time to eat the harvest

December

1

These are the socks I brought to France

I never wanted to write a breakup poem.

Let the stories collect at the nape of my neck

Let the stories collect on my skin

Let them drip
down
my
thighs

How will you commemorate the day? She asks

I won't, I say, picking at my nails. Actually, maybe I will launch my whole course on that day. Maybe I will transform the day into empowerment. Look who I have become. Look what I have done with—

Maybe nothing, she says gently

Maybe, instead, we spend the days around the day grieving. Maybe we spend three full months in sadness. Maybe your Instagram gets banned forever and the web designers fail to do their jobs on time or correctly. Maybe your whole life turns into

mixing
measuring
adding more water
chopping
wondering

Maybe, the only clear message life gives you is that it is important to rest now before the next big expansion Maybe you've figured it out and you'll need a lot of energy and skill to hold space for what you will do next

If I don't answer phone calls, won't everybody decide they don't love me anymore?
If I don't answer messages, won't people never do anything nice for me again?
If I don't post every day, won't people forget I exist?
If I don't email, won't my business stop functioning completely?

So many people
in their little boxes
going to jobs in their little boxes, boxes inside of boxes

He says he wants to talk, today.

He says he wants to talk, and that he wants us to start
over.
Let's start new. Let's have a new relationship. Let's
wipe 27 years of relationship out with one 30 minute
phone call
Let's do it so we have a clean slate for the holidays

Let me collect the stories
Let me scrape them off my tongue
Let me spit the thick yellow cells
into the sink
Let me stand up bloody and shake off sweat
begin again

I had an orgasm, and in the next moment, I see myself.
I see her as a little girl, 4 or 5 or 8 years old.

She is building houses out of popsicle sticks. She is
gluing them one at a time, trying to make them fit
together. They are not fitting together properly, but she
looks content enough.

Her hair is white-blonde, she is wearing a red shirt and
blue soft pants. She is standing on the chair so she can
reach.

I wait for a while, observing her. I am fascinated that I
get to witness myself.

I remember I am in the room with Jordan. I am both
places.
I need you to hold me and be quiet, I say. He
understands, he listens.

I look at myself. This little girl.
I sit down next to her. She looks at me.

"He said I am not good at it," she says.

I am not sure what to tell her. You are good at it, I say.
You are good.

But the truth is she is not that good, so I pause.
I realize I don't really know what to say.

It doesn't matter if you're good at it, I tell her.

The point is not to be good at it. Do you like building them?

She nods uncertainly.

I gather her into my arms. It's just supposed to be fun, I say.

But I still feel uncertain

My father called me and apologized.
My father talked to me for 100 minutes
and he printed out what I had written him, pages of
everything I felt hurt by from my entire life
He printed it out, and he sat and went through it
piece
by piece
He did not justify
He owned, and explained
And it made sense.

Can it really be that easy:
Are you ready to speak?
Are you ready to hear me?

When men apologize
And they say
I did not know how to do any better at the time
and I wish I had
and this is how I felt
and I am sorry

The entire world is healing

I don't know if it's better poetry when everything is
Broken.

But it's not broken anymore. It's all healing

January

She says, this sounds like your inner critic
She says, please write down the voice of your inner
critic.

I laugh. That's easy, I say

I fill half a page in two minutes.

Read it aloud, she says

Ok.

*You are failing at everything. Nothing you do is good enough.
Everything is going wrong and always goes wrong for you. You
are bad at everything. You can't do anything correctly—*

Tears stream down my cheeks. I feel like I'm 5.

She stops me. Well, that was about thirty seconds…
She smiles

Look down at that paper
All of those things are lies

You learned them in childhood, you absorbed them
without understanding how to tell the difference. You
made up rules to make sense of the world you were
living in, a world where you were valued for being
Good At Things and for being mean to yourself

All of these things are lies, she says
You can choose not to believe them any longer

So today, I was walking down the street
And many things did not happen in an ideal way at
once
And one thing after another was too many
And I heard that voice, wanting to jump in and say
Everything is wrong, always
Look at everything going wrong. You are not doing
well today. Nothing is going right for you.

And then I remembered she said all those things were
lies
And I said to myself, well, if those things are lies
Then what else

And I said it feels boring to choose to not feel

And he said think what else you could accomplish

I thought it seemed boring to choose to turn off my feelings. But that's not what I was doing, not really – instead I was choosing to turn off the critic, who was sending me into a spiral whenever I did anything differently than usual.

She told me that sometimes, when we go through trauma, we can become addicted to our own stress response. To the adrenaline, to the chemicals released during times of crisis.

And I thought about my brother
And I thought about how I know how to be in hospitals
And I thought about the death of my grandfather
And I thought about funerals, and how I am good at them

And then I wondered about my affinity for being in new places alone
And how I loved getting locked out of the house
And how I let my bank account get low before I move money around

Stress on purpose

The thing is, when we realize things are Learned
Only then can we unlearn them

My wish for you, Demetra, she said
Is that you acclimatize to your own sense of calm.

February

9

If you die, I will
remember
the way you said
my beautiful girl
your hands on my cheek, with wonder
your eye corners like tree branches
your deep groans
I will remember
the way your big hands traced pathways around my
body
streams, rivers, oceans
the intoxicating scent of your skin
the way my head nestled into your chest
when we stand
I will remember
the way you held me after every orgasm
and told me my pleasure nourishes you
I will remember
your giant body enclosing mine
your hands touching my butt every night
the way you watch me
how you notice me
always
I will remember
your eyes sparkling
when I cry
pulling me close
I will remember the way your face scrunched up
when I scrubbed it
and made you that awful tea
I will remember
you holding my gaze

saying my love
saying you'd love me forever
I will remember
laughing like children
on our fourth mattress in four months
giggling uncontrollably in the dark
I will remember
your puppy dog head movements
you bringing home flowers
and croissants, and smartsweets
and everything else I wanted
I will remember your expression when we talked about
moisturizer
I will remember you solving every problem
your long eyelashes
your perfect mouth

If you die, I will
not
recover

10

Daddy's friends are coming over soon
He said
Tracing the curve of my butt
smacking it

How's that pussy doing

His cock in my mouth
My knees on the hard floor

Wet, I said

He spun me around
Stand up, he said
My hands on the bench
Grabbing my hair
He entered me

You like being filled up by me, slut? He asked

Yes, Daddy

The phone rang
They're here, he said
He buzzed them up
He stayed inside me

He went faster, harder
So I was gasping
Then he removed himself
Abruptly
There was a knock on the door

Get yourself together, he said
Daddy's busy now

I laid in bed, tuned out of my body, watched the
internet

Two hours later
I opened the door to an empty home
Just him

We stopped, stared at one another

How's your body doing, he asked

I felt my shorts flood
Turned on, I said. Just by seeing you

He strode across the room
Kissed me, yanked my head back
Grabbed my breasts
Turned toward the bed, said
Lie down

He said
Does my little girl want to come?

Yes, Daddy

He turned on the vibrator
He held my body
3, 4, 5 orgasms
I yelled to god
I became god

I said
Can I get on top of you
Use the vibrator that way

We shifted
I moved around on top of him
Feeling the slipperiness
I moved him to my entrance
He filled me

He groaned, loudly
I melted

Aren't you forgetting something? He asked
I couldn't think
I grabbed the vibrator

My pussy dripping
I touched it to my clit
Moved it around
He pushed inside of me

I came, screaming
It was unending

My breasts, standing up
My back, arched
Overwhelming sensation

When I had come for so long I couldn't feel my body, I
paused, slowed
He calibrated
Still inside of me, he reached up
One hand on my upper back

One hand on my heart
Holding me together
I cried

I lay back down, on top of him
He hugged me, stroked my hair
Pushed deeper

We flipped over

I want you to come all over me, I said

He took his time

He said, you're so open
You're almost taking all of me

He growled, he fucked me intensely
Grabbing my hips, my sides
He came on my breasts, my belly
He roared

When you roar when you come I want to serve it forever. I want to bow down to it, I want to melt. I feel as though you are a wild animal capturing me and you have won, I have willingly surrendered, I have given myself to you. I will surrender to that roar, to the king of the kingdom. Take me, I think. Have me, because this sound is all I ever need to live

20

He says
Perfect breasts
Perfect mouth
Angel hair

I love your tummy
I love your face shape
I love your hands
Perfect legs
Perfect thighs
Perfect butt
Ocean eyes
Ocean pussy
I love your skin tone
I love your nose
I love your tongue
I love your little body
I love your tattoos and their placements
I love your height
I love your scars

Like affirmations, every day

I hear them in my head now, when I look in the mirror

21

Rooting isn't easy, but it has been simple

I don't forget to eat, now

I still drink mushrooms

I lie on the floor on a plushy white carpet
I sleep wrapped in soft white sheets
I say I love you during sex
We don't have a couch, just giant cushions
We cuddle, a lot

Tonight the magic of life landed upon me again
Tonight, amidst the day-to-day routine
the way it'd be easy to take it for granted
the calm felt boring
And then it shifted, and I understood

I can choose, and it never disappears
I don't need a breakup
I don't need a journey
I don't need adrenaline

A fragile pink rose snaps off in my fingers
It glows white in the moonlight
it's February, in Vancouver

I feel grateful for the amount of pleasure I can
experience in my body. My self-pleasure, that's what
reminds me constantly of who I truly am, of my true
power. My capacity for pleasure during sex, the visions
I have afterwards. The healing that happens from
sexual energy. If everyone learned to feel this in their
body, they would remember who they truly are

The voice isn't gone, not entirely, but it no longer feels
real. She says it'll disappear one day, if I keep reminding
myself not to believe it
If I keep setting boundaries with anyone who continues
it, including myself
I believe her

It feels new and interesting, to notice what I can do
without believing the voice

Because if all of it has always been a lie
...

acknowledgements

thank you to jordan gray for loving me in such a way that i learned how to love more deeply than i ever have in my entire life. thank you for your endless support, for falling in love with my poems, for falling in love with my mind. thank you for the pleasure you bring me, for the ways you make my life easy, for your thoughtfulness and humor and the way you touch me. thank you to vancouver for your rain and beautiful nature and your sense of safety. thank you to patricia culver for seeing me so fully and providing me with exactly what i needed exactly when i needed it. thank you to my family; knowing i have your unending love is vital. thank you to everyone in my patreon for giving me a space to share these pieces as they were created. and thank you to bethany, casey, ellie, lily, mackenzie, and molly for being such support systems full of laughter and understanding.

I love you

ABOUT THE AUTHOR

Demetra Nyx is a sex coach, writer, and creator who lives in Vancouver. You can see the rest of her art and learn about her online course, Falling in Love with Yourself, by visiting demetranyx.com.

Made in the USA
San Bernardino, CA
25 March 2020